Ambulance in Action

Peter Bently

Illustrated by Martha Lightfoot

Ambulance and its crew are in
the **ambulance station**.

Ambulance has lots of **special equipment**.
Meerkat and Ambulance Driver are checking it all.

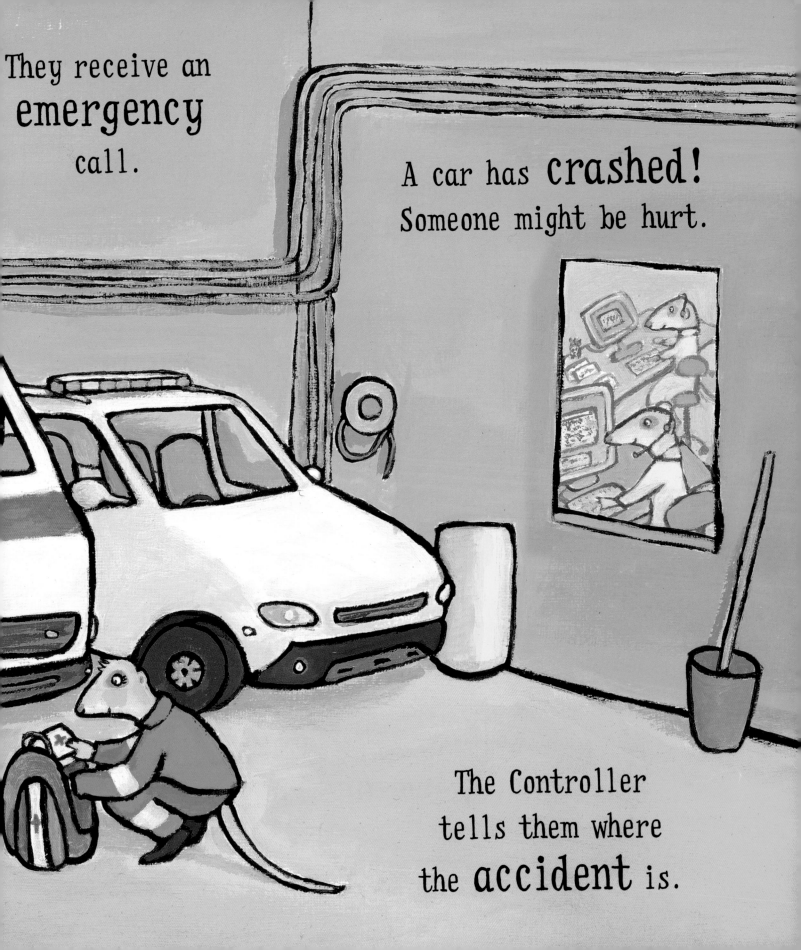

They receive an **emergency** call.

A car has **crashed!**
Someone might be hurt.

The Controller
tells them where
the **accident** is.

Meerkat and Ambulance Driver jump
into Ambulance and **shut** the doors.

CLUNK!

They put on their **seat belts.**
Ambulance Driver quickly checks the radio
for the location, and sets the satnav.

VRRROOM!

Then he turns the ignition key. Ambulance's big engine **roars** into life. They are on their way. There's **no time to lose!**

Ambulance **speeds** along the road.

Oh no, look at that traffic jam!
Ambulance Driver switches on the siren
and the warning lights.

Ambulance reaches the **accident**. The police are already there and have stopped the traffic.

Meerkat grabs her first aid bag and *leaps* out of Ambulance.

The car driver has hurt his leg.
He thinks it is bro ken.

Meerkat cannot get to
him because the car door
won't open.

Ambulance Driver radioes the
controller who tells him the
Fire Service are on their way.

Ambulance Driver gets the **stretcher** out of Ambulance and lowers the ramp.

He is getting everything **ready** while they wait for the Fire Service.

Meerkat stays with the car driver.

The fire crew use a special **cutting tool**.
Very **carefully**, they cut off the car door.

Meerkat and Ambulance Driver **lift**
the car driver onto the stretcher.

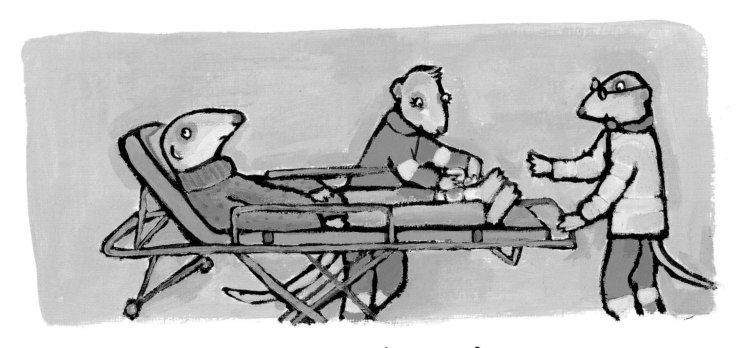

Meerkat puts a **dressing** on
the car driver's leg and **straps** it up.

Ambulance's crew **wheel** the stretcher into the back of Ambulance.

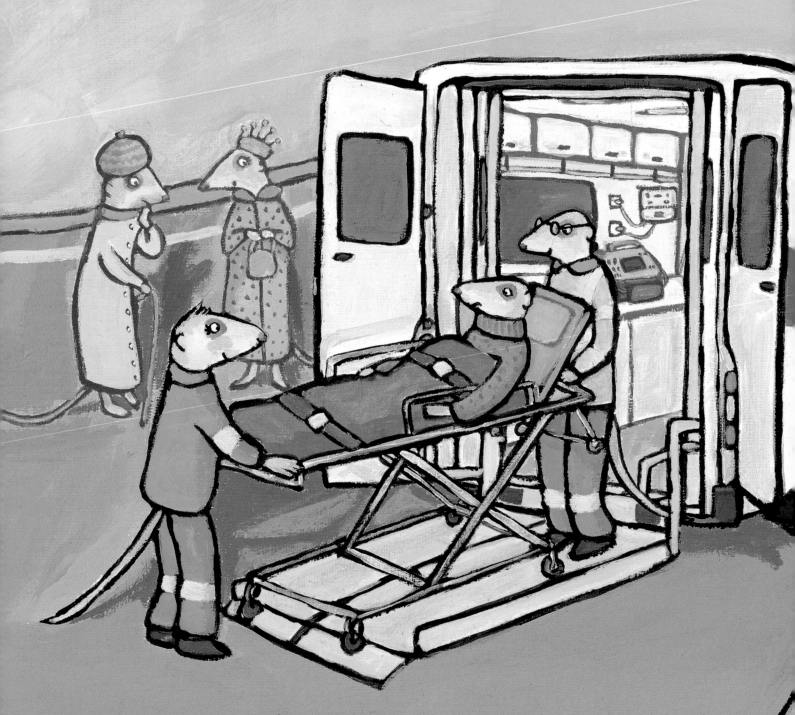

Meerkat **fixes** the stretcher in place.

WHIRR! CLUNK!

Then she **raises the ramp** and **shuts** Ambulance's door.

Meerkat sits in the **back** with the car driver.

Meerkat tells him **not to worry**.
He is going to be fine.

Ambulance reaches the **hospital** very quickly.
The hospital staff are waiting.

The car driver **thanks** Ambulance's crew.

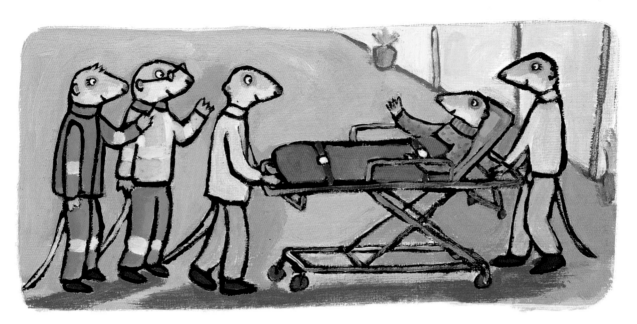

"Well done, Ambulance!" says Meerkat.
"You deserve a rest!"

Then her radio goes **beep-beep!**
"Sorry Ambulance, it's another emergency.
We must hurry!"

Let's look at
Ambulance

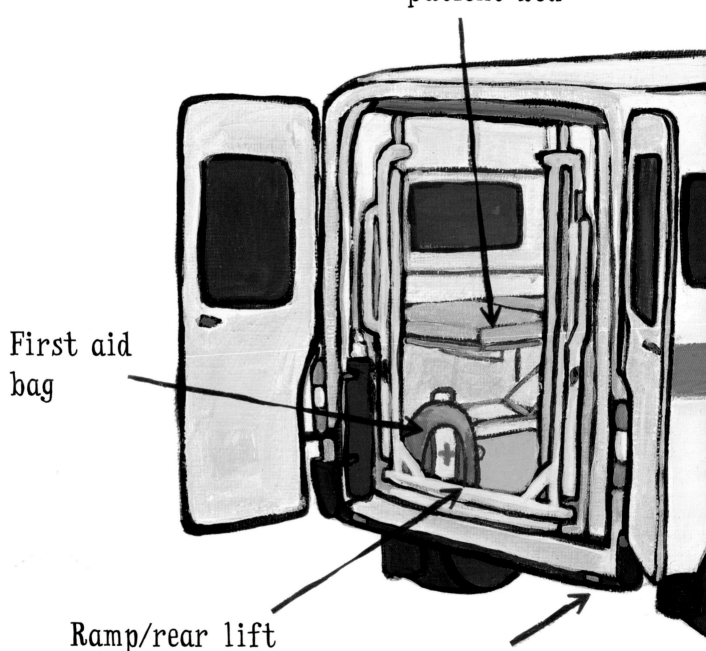

Wheeled stretcher/
patient bed

First aid
bag

Ramp/rear lift

Rear lights

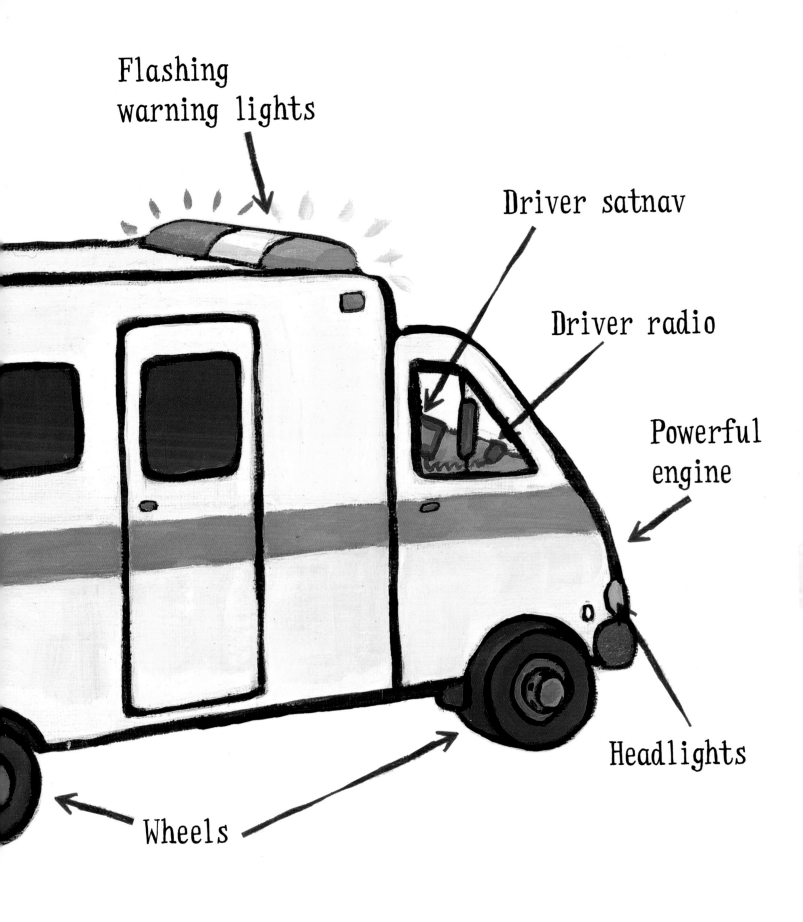

Other Emergency Vehicles

Fire engine

Police car

Air ambulance

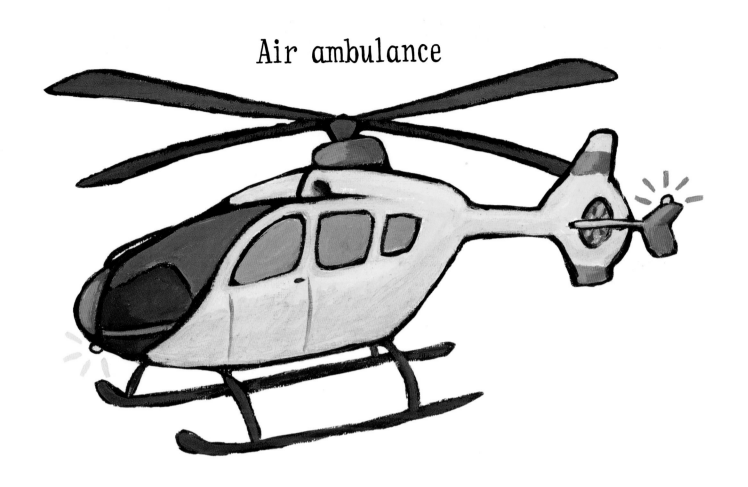

Police motorcycle

For my granny, Peggy, with thanks. M.L.
For Eli. P.B.

Quarto is the authority on a wide range of topics.

Quarto educates, entertains and enriches the lives of our readers—enthusiasts and lovers of hands-on living.

www.quartoknows.com

Designer: Plum5 Limited
Project Editor: Lucy Cuthew
Editorial Assistant: Tasha Percy

First published in the UK in 2013 by QED Publishing
Part of The Quarto Group
The Old Brewery, 6 Blundell Street
London, N7 9BH

A catalogue record for this book is available from the British Library.

ISBN: 978 1 78171 801 8

Printed in China